HOW THEY LIVED

The GREEKS

NEIL GRANT

MALLARD PRESS

Remains of the 4th-century B.C. Ionic temple of Athena at Priene in Asia Minor (now Turkey). Athena was the goddess of Athens, but she was worshipped all over the Greek-speaking world.

Contents

Introduction

The age of Classical Greece, the foundation of European civilization, began about the beginning of the 5th century B.C. and ended before the end of the 4th century. That is not a long time – less than 200 years – but of course it cannot be seen in isolation. Greek civilization was in existence 300 years earlier, and Greek culture in one form or another dominated the Mediterranean region for centuries afterwards; it continues to influence us today.

The earliest civilization on mainland Greece was the Bronze Age civilization known as Mycenaean, after the city where the most spectacular remains were found by archaeologists in the last century. Mycenaean civilization, itself preceded by Minoan civilization in Crete, disappeared round about 1200 B.C. Its decline roughly coincided with invasion by a wilder, Greek-speaking race from the north called the Dorians. No doubt they were partly responsible for the disappearance of Mycenaean civilization, though there seem to have been other causes.

The period of about four centuries that followed is known as the Dark Age, partly because records of it are few and our knowledge of the period is therefore slight. Since

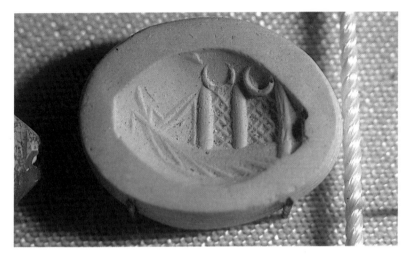

it coincided with the introduction of iron, which replaced bronze as the main metal for tools and weapons, the Dark Age cannot be dismissed as a period of cultural retreat. However, there were no great stone buildings or works of art as the Mycenaeans had produced, and – a significant indicator of civilization – the art of reading and writing was lost.

What we call Classical Greek civilization began to develop in the 8th century B.C. According to tradition, the first Olympic Games were held about 776 and, more important, the poet Homer (possibly not just one person) composed his epics, the *Iliad* and the *Odyssey*, works that were to gain the status almost of holy books among later generations, in the second half of the 8th century.

The early period of Greek civilization (from about 700 to 500 B.C.) is known as the Archaic Age. There were great advances in science, literature and the arts, though Greek works were heavily influenced by the older cultures of the Near East and Egypt.

In the 5th century B.C., with the defeat of the Persians in protracted wars which had compelled the Greek states to fight as one people in face of a greater enemy, Classical Greece finally emerged. In our eyes, the change was rather sudden, at least in the arts: the stiff, "oriental" statues of Apollo vanished, to be replaced almost instantly by the serenely harmonious ideal of the human body which still inspired artists living 2,000 years later.

The unity achieved in the Persian wars did not last long. The leading Greek powers, Sparta (primarily military) and Athens (naval as well as cultural), fell out. Athenian empire-building antagonized many of her former allies, and the Peloponnesian War (perhaps the most discussed war in history before the 20th century) ended in the defeat of Athens and led, at the end of the 5th century, to a period of dominance by Sparta.

A new power arose in the 4th century – Macedon, largely Greek in culture though of mixed race, lacking the democratic traditions of Greek states, ruled by hereditary kings and regarded by the Greeks as rather barbarous. Under an ambitous new dynasty Macedon expanded, gaining control of Greece and, under Alexander the Great (356–323), creating an empire which extended to the limits of the known world.

Minoan seals (strictly, impressions of the seals in plaster) of (right) a ship and (left) a pair of goats, from the 18th century B.C.

The Greek State

Land and People

Greece is a mountainous country with deep valleys, large sea gulfs but few rivers, and many islands. It is a small country, and not very well blessed with natural resources. There were more trees in ancient times, but even then pastures rich enough for cattle were not common. The climate is dry, though clear and healthy (the smog of Athens is a very recent development).

Though Nature was hard and life not easy, many Greeks seem to have lived to a great age, even by modern standards. Sophocles was still writing plays at 90, King Agesilaus of Sparta still going to war at 80.

The nature of the country affected the development of Greek civilization in many ways. Every settlement was separated from its neighbours by mountains or the sea. To ship goods to a neighbouring town in the next valley, it was easier to carry them down the valley to the sea and up the next valley rather than across the mountains.

A typical Greek landscape, with rugged mountains interrupted by narrow plains and valleys.

The Greeks became sailors much as people today become car drivers. Sailing a boat was something that nearly every man could do, an everyday skill as common as milking goats or making a speech.

The formidable physical barriers between settlements made it difficult to establish central control. In earlier civilizations, which grew up along river valleys like the Nile in Egypt or the Tigris and Euphrates in Mesopotamia, a strong central government could maintain its rule easily. Thanks to the easy communications provided by the river, the whole area could be organized as one unit, with different tasks for different people. Greek settlements had

A Greek ship, from a mosaic. The magic eye painted on the bow was intended to guide the ship on the correct course, or perhaps keep evil spirits away.

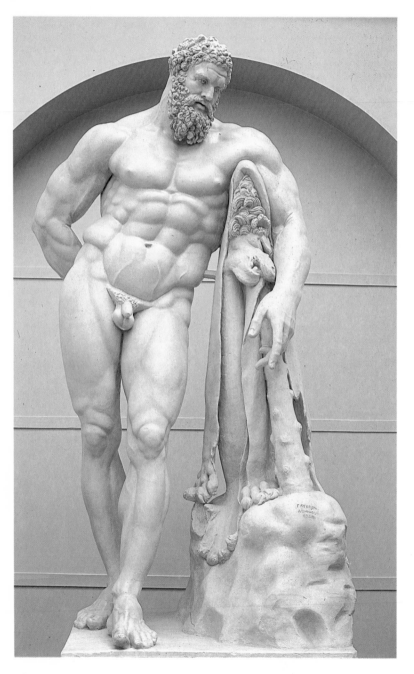

to be more independent, and their inhabitants had to be skilled in a wider range of tasks. Specialization was a luxury the Greeks could not usually afford. Moreover, they liked living in small communities and viewed a huge state like the Persian Empire with disapproval.

These conditions nourished the qualities for which we admire the ancient Greeks today, notably their belief in the importance of the individual. The earlier, "Eastern" civilizations were ruled by a monarch so autocratic that he was almost, if not entirely, a god. The people he ruled were mere tools for carrying out his will. To the Greeks, this was barbaric. While they did not believe that all men – let alone all human beings – are equal, they did believe that a man must be respected as an individual, and that his aim in life should be to fulfil his own destiny – we might say, to be himself. In the words of the great Athenian statesman, Pericles, "Every one of our citizens, in all the many aspects of life [is] the rightful lord and owner of his own person."

From this came the Greeks' love of freedom. They did not like being told what to do, whether by Persians or anyone else. A man needed to be free to fulfil his own potential. He should be able to say what he thought and to go where he liked. With this went a deep respect for personal honour. For all the intellectual brilliance of Athens, the Greeks put honour before intelligence. The most popular of their mythical heroes was Heracles (Hercules), a figure noted more for his brawn than his brain. They were less sure about Odysseus, a rare figure among Greek heroes since his exploits depended on intelligence, even trickery, rather than straightforward effort.

These beliefs no doubt developed in a vague instinctive way, but they became the basis of Greek philosophy, that great body of thought which is the subject of as much debate in today's universities as it was in 5th-century B.C. Athens.

The Polis

Polis, from which we get our word politics, was the Greek name for the community which, for lack of a better translation,we call a city-state. The most notable feature of these political units is that they were very small. The philosopher Aristotle said that all the citizens of the polis ought to know each other by sight. Plato thought that 5,000 citizens was about the right number. Some were much smaller than that.

This figure, however, excluded women and children, slaves and foreigners, and so the total population would be larger. Athens, probably the largest city in Greece, had about 20,000 citizens in the 5th century, out of a total population of about 350,000. Attica (the total territory of Athens) was the size of an average English county, though Sparta, with fewer citizens, was much larger in area. Mycenae, no longer a great city, had an army of only 80 men. Nevertheless, like the hundreds of other city-states, Mycenae was independent. The Greeks were a "nation" only in the sense that they spoke the same language and shared many of the same customs and beliefs. They were not a nation in the modern political sense, and usually expressed deep dislike for such an idea.

Towns grew up around a citadel, or acropolis, which was often (as in Athens) a high point, easily defended. Besides the town itself, where most people lived, the city-state consisted of the surrounding villages and agricultural land necessary to support the townspeople.

The polis was more than just a government, it was also "the people". The government might be run by a king, or a group of nobles, or by a council of citizens, but it was a government of the people (at least, the citizens). Its justification for its existence was that it ensured justice and enforced the law – not through courts and judges but through the people. If someone had a complaint, he obtained justice by making his complaint known to the people, who were all involved in public life. Because the community was such a small one, everyone knew, more or less, what everyone else was up to. This would be impossible in a modern society where any one person, whether banker or plumber, secretary or hairdresser, knows almost nothing about the work and lives of his neighbours.

The polis was, therefore, at once state and nation, government and people. In fact it was even more than all that. It was a way of life, including the arts, religion and social life. It was society as a whole, more like a large family than a political organization.

The Acropolis, or citadel, of Athens, which in Classical times became a sanctuary rather than a fort. The splendid buildings, which have partly survived wars, robbers and greedy art collectors, were mostly built in the time of Pericles.

Athenian Democracy

Ruled in earlier times by kings, groups of nobles or by rulers known as tyrants (not such a sinister name then as it is now), in the 5th century Athens had a democratic form of government which was copied by many other city-states, especially those which were part of Athens's recently acquired empire.

The most important body was the assembly, which included all adult male citizens. Here all matters of policy and law-making were discussed, and officials were elected. In theory, anyone could speak on any matter, though in practice it was not so easy because of the sheer size of the membership. At least 6,000 had to be present before serious decisions could be taken, and a citizen was expected, though not forced, to attend.

ILLYRIA

MACEDONIA

● Therma
(Thessalonica)

M. Olympus ▲

THRACIAN SEA

TROAD
Ilium (Troy)

PHRYGIA

KORKYRA
(CORFU)

THESSALY

LYDIA

ITHACA   Delphi ●

● Ephesus

● Thebes

Corinth ●   ● Athens

AEGEAN SEA

PELOPONNESE ● Mycenae ATTICA

Argos ●   ● Epidauros

Olympia ●

ARCADIA   THE CYCLADES

Sparta
●

LACONIA

RHODES

IONIAN SEA

MEDITERRANEAN SEA   CRETE

Knossos
●

The boundaries of the
Greeks' universe
stretched not much
further than the
shores of the Aegean,
Homer's 'wine-dark
sea'.

Most of the preparatory work was done by a council of 500 citizens, who were elected for a year at a time by the assembly and represented equally the ten tribes into which the citizens of Athens were divided. Much routine business was carried on by a smaller committee.

The most powerful individuals in the state were the ten "generals" (the Greek word could also be translated "admirals"). As the name suggests, their original job was to command the armed forces. They too were elected by the assembly for a year's office, but they could be re-elected the following year and often were. (Others, however, could find themselves a general one year and a private soldier the next.) It was through holding this office, besides his personal qualities of leadership, that Pericles became so dominant a figure in Athens from 460 to 429 B.C., and from that time onwards the generals became the chief state officials, or ministers, as well as military commanders.

Other officials were chosen by lot. Simple machines were used for this purpose, with black and white wax balls indicating whether a particular man should serve or not (the origin of our expression "black-balled"). Juries were also chosen in this way. There was no judge and no professional lawyers. The accused spoke in his own defence, though he might have prepared his speech with the help of a professional speechwriter.

As even the poorest citizen might find himself chosen to serve in public office, all civil servants, jurors and other officials were paid out of state funds to make up for their loss of earnings. A rich citizen, however, was expected to provide some extra public service – for example, by paying for a warship (in which case he was entitled to command the ship in battle).

The assembly was supreme, and there were excellent safeguards against bribery and corruption and to prevent an ambitious man from seizing power. A politician who showed a tendency in that direction was likely to be "ostracized" – sent into exile for ten years – by vote of the assembly.

Athenian democracy has been greatly admired down the centuries. It was certainly more democratic than many modern democracies, and it was remarkably free of corruption. Though the vote of the assembly could be influenced by a powerful orator, it worked remarkably well on the whole. It was deliberately – and in our eyes surprisingly – non-professional. Government and administration were part of the everyday life of the citizen, just as much as earning a living or family life. The Athenians certainly made some bad, sometimes disastrous, judgments. But professional politicians have been known to make mistakes too! The system worked as well as it did, first, because the state was so small and, second, because life was comparatively simple .

However, Athenian democracy was not the near-perfect system that some romantically minded historians used to think. Although the assembly was supreme, and all male citizens were members of it, they represented only a small proportion (about one-sixth) of the population of Athens. Those who had no vote in the assembly included all women, all those of non-Athenian birth and – the largest group – slaves.

Nor was the Athenian system universal. Athens's great rival, Sparta, was an entirely different type of state, ruled by a small class, with a large, oppressed population of serfs (helots), an assembly where no real debate was possible, and a rigid, reactionary society organized on puritanical, militaristic lines. The Spartan system has some virtues of its own – many Greeks admired it (the word 'Spartan' is still used today to denote the ability to bear pain) – but the extraordinary string of geniuses who lived in Classical Greece flourished not in Sparta but in the freer society of Athens.

At Work and at Home

Farming

As in all early civilizations, the most important economic activity in ancient Greece, and the one which employed by far the greatest number of people, was farming. Good farming land in Greece is scarce because of the dry climate and the mountainous landscape, and it was the shortage of land which prompted the Greeks to found colonies around the Mediterranean (as far west as Spain) and the Black Sea during the Archaic period.

The dry summers and poor soil made it impossible to grow enough corn, and in Athens about two-thirds of the grain needed to make bread was imported from the Black Sea region and other places. Olives and grapes (for wine) on the other hand grew well in most places and olive oil was one of Athens's chief exports. The main vegetables were beans, peas, lentils, onions, cabbages and lettuce. Goats were kept for their milk and sheep mainly for their wool. Both could graze on the lower slopes of mountains, but good grazing for cattle was scarce outside Thessaly in the north-east. Donkeys and mules provided transport and the meat most often eaten came from pigs and young goats. As sugar was unknown, bees were kept for their honey. Mount Hymettus in Attica was famous for its honey, and archaeologists have recently discovered there the remains of beehives made of terracotta (earthenware). Some of them still contained traces of beeswax.

Farming methods in Classical Greece were rather simple, though many improvements came during the Hellenistic period, when Alexander's conquests introduced the Greeks to new crops, animals and techniques.

The plough was the old type which had been in use without much change for many centuries. It was little more than a thick

spike, attached to a handle held by the ploughman, and a pole fixed to a yoke. It did not turn the soil, but made a furrow in which the seed was sown. In later times, wheels were added. The grain was harvested with sickles and threshed on a threshing floor by mules or donkeys driven around in a circle. After being threshed and

Olives were a valuable crop. They are easily bruised and were often gathered by shaking or knocking the branches, as in this scene on a black-figure vase of the 4th century B.C.

15

A pastoral scene, with the rustic god Pan playing his pipe, from a mosaic of the 2nd century A.D. in Corinth.

Blacksmiths working at the anvil. This was a vital craft with its own blacksmith-god, Hephaestos.

winnowed, the grain was ground into flour by hand with a mortar and pestle. Different crops were grown on a field for two years, and the third year it was left fallow. Because horses and cattle were scarce, manure was in short supply.

Olives were harvested by knocking the branches with a stick, and crushed in a press to extract the oil. To make wine, grapes were first trampled by human feet, to the sound of music, then squeezed in a press, and the juice allowed to ferment.

Farming land was usually owned privately, and although large estates existed in some parts, most farms were small. Peasant farmers had to work very hard, especially at seed-time and harvest. However, on larger farms, and in later times on some smaller ones too, the hard work was done by slaves.

Slaves

All early civilizations had slaves, and it is hard for us to understand how the Greeks, with their love of personal freedom, could have tolerated slavery. Of course, life in general was harder and more brutal in ancient times, and people accepted many things which we should find intolerable today. More important, though, slavery was a less brutal institution than the kind of slavery that developed, for example, in the Americas 2,000 years later. The position of slaves in ancient Greece was more like that of serfs in medieval Europe than Africans on the tobacco and cotton plantations of the New World in the early 19th century.

One important fact was that most slaves were prisoners-of-war, and were people of the same racial background as their owners. They could not be thought of as members of an "inferior" race. They had more freedom and more legal protection than slaves in the Americas (or in the Roman empire for that matter). Spartans used to sneer that in Athens you could not tell the difference between a slave and a citizen.

There were even some advantages in being a slave. Life could be quite comfortable for a slave in domestic service – as about half the slaves in Athens were – if it were a kindly household. Also, slaves did not serve in the army or navy, and might one day gain their freedom.

However, some slaves did live in terrible conditions. One of the black marks on the record of Athens is the use of slaves in the mines and quarries. A man sent to work in the mines often stayed there until he died, and, working on all fours or lying on his back in a narrow tunnel, he often died rather quickly.

Industry

Slaves also worked in other industries, which were much smaller in scale than mining and quarrying. Crafts is a better word than industry, because the typical "factory" was a workshop run by a family of craftsmen – shoemakers, metalworkers, weavers, potters and so on – helped by a few slaves. Larger establishments were uncommon until Hellenistic times, and they did not have many labour-saving "machines", because as labour was cheap there was no need to invent such devices.

A cobbler's shop, carved in relief on a tomb of the 4th century B.C.

Pottery

Pottery was important to the Greeks because it was used for storing food and drink. It is even more important to us because it was painted with scenes from everyday life or from Greek mythology, and provides us with much valuable information.

This kind of pottery is divided into two main types. In "black-figure" pottery, which originated in Corinth but was taken up by Athens, the figures are black against the lighter background of the clay. It was first made about 700 B.C. and continued until the invention of "red-figure" pottery in the 6th century. Red-figure pottery was made from reddish clay, and the background was painted black so that the fig-ures stood out in the natural colour of the clay.

The Athenian potters shaped the vessel on a wheel, turned by an apprentice (often the potter's son). The vessel was then kept in a damp room until ready for the painter, who might be the potter himself but often was not. We know many painters by name, because they signed their work. After painting, the vessel was "fired" in a kiln. This process of baking the clay until it was hard required great skill and experience.

Vessels of pottery were turned out in their hundreds, in a large number of well-known shapes, with names like *krater*, *amphora*, etc. They were of course practical objects, made to be used. But to us they appear among the finest works of European art.

Below right: A black-figure ewer, or jug, of the 5th century B.C.

Below left: A red-figure *krater* with a scene of an incident in mythology in which Heracles and Apollo quarrelled over possession of a sacred tripod at Delphi.

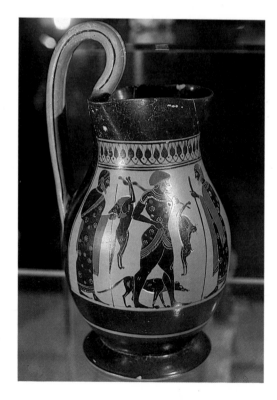

Trade and Ships

The richest cities in ancient Greece were those that had good harbours. Piraeus, the port of Athens, was one of the best. Most trade was done by private merchants in their own ships. They would sail to several ports on a long voyage, buying what was cheap in a certain place and selling what was expensive, and paying a small charge in customs duties to the state. Although barter – exchanging one sort of goods for another – still went on, the Greeks did much of their business in cash. This did not necessarily make things simpler because each city-state issued their own coins (mostly silver) and the weight, and therefore the value, varied from place to place. However, the coins of the big trading states like Athens were accepted nearly everywhere.

A vast number of products were traded. As we have seen, Athens had to import much grain. In exchange, it sold olive oil and manufactures such as pottery, cutlery and furniture. Athens also imported timber, minerals like iron and copper, animal hides, wine, dyes, papyrus (used for making paper) and hundreds of other things.

Greek ships relied on oars or sails or both. Athenian naval power was based on the trireme, a warship with three rows of oars, one above the other. Sailing ships were mostly square-rigged, a good system with a following wind but not much good for sailing into the wind. It seems that some ships did have fore-and-aft rig (sails parallel to the keel), though they were uncommon. Some merchant ships were very large. One designed by the famous inventor Archimedes in the 3rd century B.C. could carry nearly 2,000 tonnes.

Sea voyages were dangerous. Sailors usually tried to keep close to the land and ran their ships ashore for the night. Though the Mediterranean is a fairly calm sea, it is subject to sudden storms and has many dangerous passages around the

A merchant ship of the 1st century B.C., carved on a tomb.

coasts, so that shipwreck was not uncommon. (Some of the greatest archaeological "finds" of recent years have come from wrecked ships that have been preserved on the seabed for over 2,000 years). Summer was the sailing season. As far as possible, ships did not venture into the open sea in winter.

Pirates could be another danger. In Homer's time piracy was common and there was not much to choose between a merchant and a pirate. A captain and crew might set out with a shipload of goods to sell. But if they came upon a badly guarded settlement, they might decide that an armed raid would be more profitable. However, by the 5th century things had become more orderly, and Athenian ships had cleared most of the pirates out of the Aegean Sea.

Travel by land was no safer than by sea. Pirates might lurk off the coast, but bandits were just as likely to lurk in the mountain passes.

19

20

Homes and Families

As everyone knows, the Greeks built magnificent temples and palaces of limestone and marble, but ordinary houses were less grand. Houses were usually built of bricks made from mud dried in the sun, with tiled roofs. The rooms were arranged around an open courtyard, sometimes with a well or fountain. Otherwise, water had to be fetched in jars from a public fountain or a stream. There were rather primitive lavatories and, not having soap, the Greeks cleaned themselves with plain water or with oil or fuller's earth, which they then scraped off with an instrument called a *strigil*. In many houses, bedrooms were on an upper floor. Men and women slept and often ate separately.

Furniture was scanty. People lay on couches not only to sleep but also to eat. Tables were three-legged, and there was a variety of stools (less often chairs) and chests for storing clothes. Objects like musical instruments hung on the walls which were often painted with a decorative frieze or band running around the room.

One of the questions that modern experts argue about most fiercely is the position of women in ancient Greece. As in nearly all other societies of that time, the man was the boss, and women lived a much more restricted life. Legally, they were second-class citizens. They could not vote in the assembly. They could not own property or carry out legal business. A woman was under the control of her husband (who was chosen for her by her father) or, if she were unmarried, of her nearest male relative. If she was single and inherited money when her father died, she could be forced to marry a male relative to keep the fortune in the family, and he was allowed to divorce his own wife in order to marry the heiress.

All this seems disgracefully unfair. And besides the legal restrictions, women were limited in other ways. They were expected to spend their time in the house. There was

Opposite: One of the stories about the god Dionysus relates how he was captured by pirates who, when they found they had a god on board, jumped into the sea and were turned into porpoises, or dolphins, which have been friendly towards people ever since.

This sculpture of a mother and her child was carved on a stele, an upright, monumental stone like a gravestone, in the 5th century B.C.

certainly plenty to do there, because tasks like grinding corn into flour and spinning and weaving wool into cloth were normally done at home. But the wife did not even get out to do the shopping, or at least not always. Husbands did it, sending their purchases home with a servant while they went on to meet their friends or supervise the workers on their farm. (People tended to live in the city and "commute" – it wasn't far – to the farmland outside it.)

The legal restrictions on women do not tell us what family life was really like. Evidence from vase paintings and tombstones

A woman spinning yarn, from a 5th-century white-ground vessel of a kind that was often placed as an offering in tombs.

Education

They did not, however, go to school. Only boys (and only the sons of citizens) did that. They learned reading, writing and arithmetic, poetry, music and gymnastics. The Greeks considered training the body as important as training the mind. This does not mean that Greek women were uneducated, and could not read or write. They probably learned at home, though their chief studies consisted of domestic work. We should also remember that reading and writing were less important than talking and listening in Greek society, and books were rare and precious.

At school boys used wax tablets for their lessons. They wrote with a stylus, a pointed instrument, on a wooden board coated with wax. The marks could be rubbed out, the wax smoothed over, and the tablet used again.

Schooling normally ended at fifteen, probably earlier for many poorer boys as fees were charged. Informal "universities" also existed for further education, the most famous being Plato's Academy, named after the Grove of Academia, where young men met to learn the art of argument and debate. At eighteen, when a boy became a full citizen, he did two years "national service" in the army.

Our knowledge of all aspects of Greek society, including education, comes mainly from Athens. Although Athens set a standard followed by many other states, things were, once again, very different in Sparta.

The education of Spartan boys makes even the fiercest Victorian school look like a holiday camp! The Spartans were meant to be tough. At seven, boys went to boarding schools where they were allowed few clothes, no shoes, no beds and little food. They were encouraged to steal food to teach them to be quick and crafty, and they were savagely beaten for no reason except to teach them to endure pain. Their games were mostly war games, their music patri-

shows loyalty and affection in families, and literature shows that women were respected by men. It seems unlikely that Greek women felt seriously oppressed, certainly no more than women in 19th-century Britain, for example. There are plenty of powerful female characters in Greek drama and mythology. Nor is it true that women were shut away indoors like nuns in a monastery. We know that they went to the theatre, we hear of them visiting friends, and they also took part in the sports and games of which the Greeks were so fond.

otic songs and marches. Even girls (who did not go to school) were expected to be tough, and good wrestlers.

When talking about Classical Greece, it is easy to see Athens in a rosy glow of virtue and Sparta in a black cloud of rigid severity. But things were not so clear-cut. Spartan children were taught to respect older people, and Spartan women were legally freer than Athenian women.

A modern engraving depicting the training of Spartan schoolboys.

Clothes

The Greeks wore loose, simple clothes. The gown worn by women was called a *chiton* and consisted of a large rectangle of cloth, finely woven and made at home, which was passed around the body, fixed at the shoulders with pins, gathered at the waist with a girdle, and allowed to fall in folds. Cloaks or mantles were worn on top when outdoors. Men wore a similar loose tunic, which might be short (above the knee) or full-length. Sometimes they wore a gown which consisted, like the *chiton*, of one piece of cloth, looped over one shoulder and gathered at the waist, or a simple cloak called a *chlamys*. The climate was usually warm, and as the Greeks were not ashamed of the human body, men and boys wore nothing at all when taking part in athletics. Outdoors, stout sandals, some of them more like boots, were worn, but indoors people mostly went barefoot. Men sometimes wore rather modern-looking broad-brimmed hats, especially (so it seems from pictures on pottery) when travelling, and sometimes they wore cone-shaped caps.

Greek women grew their hair long, but did it up in a large variety of styles, held in place with head bands. Wigs and dyed hair were not unknown among women of prosperous households, and they also used make-up to whiten their faces, redden their lips and emphasize their eyes. Many beautiful little jars and boxes for powder and perfumes have been found in tombs.

The Greeks were expert metalworkers, and their gold jewellery – head bands, bracelets, necklaces, ear rings and brooches – displays skill and taste of the highest standard. They used enamel to add colour, but not (or not often) precious stones, until the conquests of Alexander introduced them to diamonds and other gem stones. Men in Classical Greece did not wear jewellery, except sometimes a head band, and usually grew beards after a certain age.

Sport and Games

The Greeks believed in plenty of exercise. Children played many vigorous games with balls (the earliest description of a ball game is in Homer's *Odyssey*), hoops, carts, etc. Men went frequently to the public gymnasium for exercise, perhaps a friendly wrestling match, as well as a gossip. They also played team games. One carving in stone shows a game which looks very much like two players bullying off at hockey. In their quieter moments, people could play board games, one of which seems to have been much like draughts.

Rougher sports included cock-fighting and chariot racing. Regular athletic meetings, of which the Olympic Games is best known, took place all over Greece. To begin with, their purpose was religious, to honour the gods (Olympia was the home of the gods), and they included events familiar to us today, such as the pentathlon. The origin of the modern Marathon race, however, was the exploit of a runner who carried the news of the battle of Marathon to Athens in 490 B.C. a distance of about 23 miles. Today the race is run over 26 miles 385 yards.

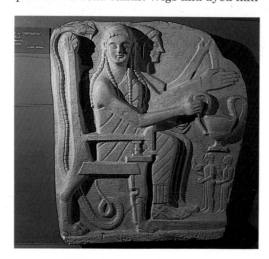

This Archaic (6th century B.C) sculpture, known as the Crysapha stele, shows that long pigtails were fashionable at that time.

A game that looks very much like modern field hockey, from the base of a statue in Athens, about 500 B.C.

Athletes practising with discus and javelin, from a 4th-century B.C. Attic vase.

Entertainment

Music seems to have been very important to the Greeks, and it is unfortunate that we do not know what it sounded like. Two of the most popular instruments were the lyre, a stringed instrument played like the harp, and the pipes.

The Greeks had many ways to amuse themselves. Besides the gymnasium, men could also go to the public baths, which was more like a club, or to the barber's shop, if they wanted a gossip as well as a haircut. Musicians, acrobats and others sometimes performed in the streets, and they were hired for private dinner parties where a lot of wine was drunk and pretty girl dancers and musicians entertained the guests. There might be women guests too, but not (as a rule) wives.

Public entertainments were mostly connected with religious festivals. Prizes could be won for reciting poetry, singing and dancing or playing an instrument, as in athletic contests. Greek drama (see page 32) also developed at these festivals, most of which were local celebrations though some, like the Panathenaia at Athens, attracted visitors from all over Greece and beyond.

Religion and Mythology

The Greeks had a love of order and unity, which lay behind their artistic and intellectual achievements, but their religion seems at first sight very disorderly, with a bewildering number of gods and goddesses. And the powerful Greek belief in morality and honour seems to be absent in their religion and mythology, where one would expect it to be strongest. Stories about the gods contain countless examples of irresponsible behaviour, foolishness, cruelty and injustice. However, a lot of these stories were invented at a late period, when the gods no longer commanded great respect. Most of our ideas of Greek gods come from writers like Ovid, whose interests were literary, not religious (and who was not even a Greek).

In prehistoric times, every little place had its own special god, or gods. If new people arrived in the region, they brought their own gods with them. But they also worshipped the gods they found already established there, and as time went by stories would be made up to connect the old gods with the newcomers. For example, if one were a goddess and the other a god, people would come to believe that they were man and wife.

This explains why Zeus, who became the chief god among the Greeks, had so many love affairs with goddesses, nymphs and human women. The stories of his love affairs were necessary to account for the vast number of his children.

The Gods

Like other ancient civilizations, the Greeks tried to explain how things came to be as they are. In the beginning was Chaos, from which came Mother Earth, who produced Sky (Uranus). Together, Earth and Sky produced Night and Day as well as many other supernatural creatures who represented the forces of nature and also feelings

or emotions. Order was gradually introduced, first by the son of Uranus, Cronus, then with the overthrow of Cronus by his son Zeus, the father of gods and of men. With Zeus and his immediate family at the top, the innumerable myths arose as the Greeks, great story-tellers, developed explanations for everything in human terms.

Their human character is the most striking characteristic of the Greek gods and goddesses. They may have supernatural powers, but essentially they behave like human beings. They enjoy human pleasures, like eating and drinking, works of art, athletic contests, etc. Zeus is the husband with an eye for pretty girls, while Hera is his jealous wife. Aphrodite (goddess of

A bronze statue of Poseidon (or possibly Zeus) which was found in the sea in 1928 and is now in the National Museum, Athens.

love) is married to Hephaestos (the blacksmith-god) but has an affair with the virile Ares (god of war). In their home on Mount Olympus, the gods have their quarrels like any human family.

However, the gods of Olympus were not simply a superhuman version of a TV soap opera. The Greeks' religion was no less serious than other peoples'. When in later times many Greeks themselves criticized the often immoral behaviour of the gods, they missed the point. Unlike the single Gods of, say, Christianity or Islam, the Greek gods were not identified with human

morality. A god could not be expected to take a particular line of action because it was "right". It would be no more sensible to expect, say, a flash of lightning (supposed to be caused by Zeus throwing his spear) to behave in a moral way. For the gods, "good" and "bad" are irrelevant.

Nevertheless, in time the gods became the protectors of human morality. They disapproved of wrongdoers and could punish them. This made the myths in which the gods themselves behave badly hard for later, intelligent Greeks (like the philosopher Plato) to swallow. Creative writers,

especially the great tragic poets of 5th-century Athens, used the myths in their plays about human problems, often changing the story considerably in the process, and often giving to old and rather crude myths a deeper meaning.

Although the family of Olympian gods was worshipped everywhere, to some extent each state had its own special deities. For example, Ephesus was the city of Artemis, goddess of hunting. Athena was above all the goddess of Athens, having won that role in a contest with the sea-god Poseidon. Yet in different guise Athena was also worshipped in Sparta, Athens's great rival. Besides the sheer number of gods and goddesses, the more important ones took on different identities in different times and places. Hermes, the messenger-god, was also associated with trade, olive-growing, gymnastics and a large number of other activities.

The state's gods and goddesses were its guardians. If the state were defeated, its gods were defeated also. If it were destroyed, the gods died. In the story of the Trojan War, as told by Homer in the 8th century, the gods took different sides.

In the legend of the Trojan War, the Greek hero Achilles overcame the Trojan hero Hector with the aid of Athena. From a red-figure vase of the early 5th century.

Offerings, Oracles and Mysteries

The basis of Greek worship was making offerings to the gods in the form of food. Sports and festivals were also held in their honour. The temple itself, the home of the particular god, was an offering of a sort, though worship took place at an altar outside the temple. Animals were sometimes sacrificed – a male animal for gods, female for goddesses, white animals for the Olympians, dark-coloured animals for gods of the Underworld.

The purpose of these sacrifices and offerings was to please the god, who would therefore be more likely to act in the way his worshippers wanted. Poseidon would grant a safe voyage, Artemis success in the hunt.

It was sometimes possible to learn the will of the gods in advance. Omens like a dream, an eclipse of the Moon, or any

Delphi, one of the most important shrines of ancient Greece. This is the theatre with, in the background, what remains of the columns of the Temple of Apollo.

unusual happening, were thought to have a meaning, and an examination of the liver of a slaughtered animal was another way of forecasting the future. These signs were interpreted by priestly officals or professional diviners.

Oracles also foretold the future. The most famous was the oracle at Delphi, a mad old woman called Pythia whose mumblings were turned into spoken verse by the priests of Apollo. The statements of the oracle, however, were usually far from clear. Thus, when things turned out differently, the excuse could be made that the oracle's words had been wrongly interpreted.

"Mystery" religions or cults were popular because they promised happiness in the afterlife. The most famous, at Eleusis, was devoted to the worship of Demeter, the corn goddess, and her daughter Persephone, wife of Hades, god of the Underworld. The annual ceremony at Eleusis lasted over a week, during which a truce was called in any wars that happened to be going on in Greece at the time. The climax of the celebration was some kind of initiation rite, which was (and to a large extent still is) a "mystery", i.e. a secret.

Other Myths

Besides the Olympians and hundreds of minor gods and goddesses, there were also spirits of the family and the countryside, and various creatures like the nymphs, youthful female divinities who lived in woods or streams.

The Greeks had many legends about heroes and adventures of the past, which belong to folklore rather than religion. In some cases at least they were probably based on some real though long-forgotten person or event. For example, until the last century, the story of the Trojan War was thought to be just that – a story or folktale. However, we now know that there really was a city called Troy and a war between

Black-figure painting of a famous incident in the *Odyssey*, when Odysseus put out the single eye of the giant Polyphemus.

Trojans and Greeks probably did take place, not long before 1200 B.C. Odysseus (Ulysses), one of the heroes of the Trojan War whose adventures on his way back from Troy are told in the *Odyssey*, may have originally been a Mycenaean prince, like Agamemnon, Menelaus, Achilles and the others.

The most popular hero was Heracles (Hercules), who was given twelve impossible tasks to perform and completed them all. Others were Perseus, who killed the snake-haired Medusa, and Theseus, who killed the Minotaur, a monster half-man, half-bull. Theseus may once have been a real king of Athens.

The whole enormous patchwork of Greek mythology, with its complicated family relationships, its humour and savagery, and its multitude of colourful stories (many contradicting each other) was a great inspiration to writers and artists, and has remained so down to our own time.

Literature and Arts

The ancient Greeks stand at one end of the story of European civilization, and we stand at the other end. Yet in many ways the Greeks seem more "civilized" than we do.

In every kind of intellectual and artistic achievement, the Greeks were pioneers. In spite of their very limited supply of information about the world, there are few intellectual or artistic pursuits in which we do not owe something to the Greeks. Not only did they "invent" epic poetry, drama, history, philosophy, etc., their endeavours in those and many other fields reached a standard which no later age has surpassed and few have equalled.

Literature

Epic poetry begins with Homer in the 8th century B.C. Greek drama developed later, in 5th-century Athens. Greek tragedy was different from modern tragedy in many ways. It developed from the religious rites performed in religious festivals, and its theme is always connected with the relationship between mankind and the gods, the plot usually being based on myth. A large part in the play was taken by the Chorus, which comments on the plot at intervals (a device used by Shakespeare too). The actors were all male (again as were Shakespeare's), and they wore masks, which indicated their mood. The theatres were in the open air, with seats for the audience forming a semicircle around the stage and rising in tiers towards the back (they were usually built on a convenient hillside). Tickets were bronze discs, bearing the seat number.

The three greatest tragic playwrights were Aeschylus (perhaps the grandest), Sophocles and Euripides. Not all their plays have survived, though it is a marvel that so many have.

Comedies were performed as well as tragedies. Aristophanes was the great master of comedy, and as there was no censorship or laws of libel, his comedy is often strong stuff. He made extravagant fun of generals, politicians, philosophers and other great men.

The theatre at Epidaurus. Greek theatres were outdoor auditoriums, where the audience might watch three or four plays – a couple of tragedies, a comedy and a satiric play – in succession. Drama was part of social life and everyone was encouraged to attend. You could even reclaim a day's lost wages for attending.

The Greeks also originated prose fiction, although the novel did not take shape until about the 2nd century A.D., when Apuleius wrote *The Golden Ass* (written in Latin but based on old Greek stories) and an unknown author wrote the original on which the Shakespearian play *Pericles* is based. Much older are the stories known as *Aesop's Fables*, tales about animals with a moral to them, such as the story of the race between the hare and the tortoise. Aesop is supposed to have been a slave who lived in the 6th century B.C., though modern experts doubt that he existed.

The first genuine histories were also written in Classical Athens. Herodotus broke away from myths and legends, seeking out facts from documents and interviews. Thucydides, a better historian though perhaps not such a colourful writer, recorded the triumphs and disasters of the Peloponnesian War.

The Greeks produced fine lyric poets, like Pindar, and of course philosophers whose ideas have influenced European civilization so profoundly. The first of them, Socrates (died 399 B.C.), never wrote a word, but his ideas were developed by his famous pupil, Plato. A 20th-century philosopher once said that the whole of Western philosophic thought can be seen as a series of footnotes to Plato, whose *Republic* was the first attempt to describe a state run on ethical principles. Aristotle, the tutor of Alexander the Great, had an even wider-ranging mind, writing on natural science, astronomy and politics as well as logic and metaphysics. It is a striking thought that possibly no cleverer man than Aristotle, who died in 322 B.C., has ever lived.

Left: A flask in the form of an actor wearing a mask for comedy, southern Italy, 2nd century B.C.

Above: The theatre at Miletus in Asia Minor.

Architecture

The colonnaded buildings of the Greeks created what we call the Classical orders, a fundamental feature of most architectural styles ever since.

As builders the Greeks were limited in technique, knowledge and materials. Nevertheless, they produced a form of architecture which, in a building like the Parthenon, is as near perfect as anyone can imagine. Although they were poorly supplied with metals, they had large supplies of first-rate building stone, and the Parthenon is built of marble, though limestone was more common (and easier to work). Developing originally from wooden buildings, their architecture is one of straight lines, in which the central element is the column. They did not use the arch or, except occasionally, the dome, a difficult form of construction without mortar. Columns were made in sections, held together by pegs and holes in the centre of each section. Other joints were held tight with metal tags, but the main thing was to cut the stone accurately. Large stones were lifted into place with pulleys.

Boldness and simplicity were the features of Classical Greek architecture. The

A detail of the masterpiece of Greek architecture, the Parthenon in Athens.

34

In most of mainland Greece and the western colonies, the normal style was the sturdy, simple Doric (after the Dorians, who settled mainly in western Greece). In the east it was the more elegant Ionic (after the Ionians of eastern Greece). Both styles were found in Athens. The Parthenon is Doric, but shows Ionic influence, for example, in the slimness of the columns. The third Classical order, Corinthian (after the city of Corinth), with its more elaborate capital, was a later development of Ionic.

The usual plan of a Greek temple was a rectangle, with colonnades along the sides, but there were other forms, such as the *tholos*, a circular building often used for religious shrines, the *propylon*, a monumental gateway, and the *stoa*, basically a colonnade with a solid wall on one side.

Left: Ionic columns of the huge Temple of Apollo at Didyma, Asia Minor, which was the seat of a famous oracle. The temple, the greatest outside Greece, was never completely finished, but fell into ruins only after an earthquake in 1493.

Below: Detail of a Corinthian capital, which suited the taste for greater ornament in Hellenistic times.

temples and other monumental buildings were decorated with sculpture, which was always an integral part of the architecture – one could almost say the buildings are part of the sculpture.

Simplicity of plan and appearance does not mean simplicity in detail. The care taken in planning a site like the Acropolis in Athens shows keen awareness of angles, proportions and views, and the buildings themselves are much more sophisticated in design than they may appear. For example, close inspection of the Parthenon reveals that the sides of the columns have a slight convex curve – fatter in the middle than at the ends. This device, known as entasis, is designed to counter a trick played by the human eye which makes straight-sided columns look slightly concave.

Right: An early (about 490 B.C.) bronze figure of Zeus throwing his thunderbolt. King of the gods and of men, Zeus had the highest authority, and in any quarrel on Mount Olympus his judgment was final.

Opposite: A 4th-century B.C. bronze figure, more than life-size, of the goddess Athena, recovered from the sea off Piraeus. Athena was born from the head of Zeus, already wearing her helmet. The owl is a symbol of wisdom, another attribute of this formidable goddess.

Sculpture

Unfortunately, most works of ancient Greek art have long vanished. Sculpture has survived better than most, but even so it is only a tiny proportion that we are able to admire today. The favourite material of sculptors was bronze, but later ages melted down all the bronze statues they could find. The few that remain were saved because they were buried or lost at sea, to be found many centuries later when their value was better understood. However, we know roughly what many famous bronze statues looked like because we have marble copies of them made in Roman times. In general, we know the names of many sculptors in Classical Athens but have few or no examples of their work.

Luckily, sculpture from buildings (in stone) has survived better, notably the figures from the Parthenon and from the Temple of Zeus at Olympia.

The Greeks knew how to cast hollow, bronze figures in the 6th century B.C. The usual method was to make the model in wax over a clay core. This was covered with a layer of clay again and heated enough to let the wax melt out of a hole. Molten bronze was then poured into the space between the outer layer of clay and the core. When the clay mould was broken the bronze statue was revealed.

In their architecture the Greeks were searching for an ideal system in which rules of shape and proportion were perfect and unchanging. The same spirit lay behind the extraordinary works of Classical sculpture. The Greeks sought perfection in the human figure, which was also the form of the gods, and the highest form of art was therefore the human nude, chiefly the male (female nudes were rare before the 4th century B.C.).

The driving force of Greek art was therefore constantly towards greater naturalism. The early rigid statues of the gods (typically Zeus and Apollo) reflected the

influence of Mesopotamia and Egypt. In the 5th century, after the Persian invasion which seems to have acted as a spur to Greek confidence, art underwent a revolution, marked by the complete mastery of human anatomy. Poses became more relaxed. The weight of the body was often placed on one foot. Later, sculptors began to experiment with figures in action, such as the famous discus-thrower by Myron (known only from a Roman copy). The overpowering sense of dignity and grandeur which is especially characteristic of the late 5th century may have been largely due to the work of two individual geniuses, Phidias in Athens and Polyclitus of Argos. Phidias made the huge statue of Athena for the Parthenon – basically wood but covered with gold and ivory and other precious materials – which we know only from descriptions, and he was in charge of the Parthenon sculpture, often regarded as the supreme masterpiece of Classical sculpture, although others must have done the actual carving of the stone.

The feeling of religious patriotism which produced these masterpieces was fading in the 4th century, and figures began to resemble individuals rather than ideal types. Perhaps the most famous statue of this age was the Aphrodite of Cnidos by Praxiteles, who is said to have used his girlfriend as a model. Again, we know it only from copies, though we do have one genuine piece by Praxiteles, the beautiful figure of Hermes holding the baby Dionysos, found in the Temple of Hera at Olympia.

In the Hellenistic period sculpture became much more varied. Sculptors showed great virtuosity and amazing skill, and they often chose subjects which their Classical predecessors would have condemned as unworthy. In spite of many brilliant works, something of the nobility of the Classical age was lost. Nevertheless, what was lost in mobility was gained in realism.

Other Arts

In ancient Greece statues and other sculptures were painted (the paint has worn off long ago) as were wood panels on the walls of houses and tombs. Practically nothing of this survives. We can only say, from the evidence of writers and of later Roman copies, that painting was as highly developed an art in Classical Greece as sculpture. There is a story about a painter called Zeuxis whose work was so realistic that birds tried to eat his painted grapes. But almost our only evidence of Greek painting comes from pottery (see page 18).

By the end of the 5th century B.C. the Greeks had developed the art of mosaic – making pictures from black and white or coloured pebbles to make a decorative floor. Extraordinary realism was achieved with this technique, which in the 3rd century was improved by the use of cut cubes of stone, called *tesserae*. The surface of the cubes was sometimes tiny, only one or two millimetres across, and colour effects were obtained by mixing the cubes in the way some painters mix different-coloured small blobs of paint to make an overall colour different from the colours that make it up.

The Greeks were also expert metalworkers, in gold and silver especially, and commanded nearly all the techniques of later goldsmiths. They also made ornamental bronzes, sometimes gilded, and carved gems and other stones for seals (the old equivalent of a signature on documents). A late invention was the cameo, a stone carved in relief (often a human or godly head) to form an oval brooch, a type still popular now. Their sense of style, their constant search for the ideal form of things, and the skill of their craftsmen, resulted in the most ordinary objects of ancient Greece taking on what we see as great beauty. Even their coins, such as these illustrated here, are often little works of art, though the Greeks themselves would not have considered them as such.

Above: A lion hunt, in pebble mosaic (pebbles worn smooth by water were preferred), found at Pella, birthplace of Alexander the Great, and dating from about 300 B.C.

Left: Athenian gold coins of the 5th century B.C. Athenian coins like these, with the head and owl symbol of Athena, were widely used, but not until the time of Alexander the Great was a universal coinage introduced.

Opposite: Stone statue of Hippocrates, the "father of medicine" and author of the Hippocratic oath, made long after his death.

Science and Warfare

In science, as in art and architecture, the Greeks made huge advances. They were a practical people, able craftsmen and builders, and they also had a keen sense of curiosity. They wanted to find out how things were, and their fertile minds were quick to devise explanations. Their ability to formulate theories is sometimes seen as an indication of an accompanying weakness – that they were stronger on theory than on scientific experiment – but while their theories were sometimes wildly wrong, it is hardly fair to regard them as "unscientific". They used their eyes as well as their minds. Xenophanes, for example, developed a theory of geological change as a result of observing sea-shells on mountains.

The Greeks were always searching for the universal – the single cause that would explain all manner of different things. The truth, they believed, was always simple. It was just a matter of finding it, and this could be done through the power of reason.

The philosopher Thales wanted to know what the world was made of, being convinced that it was one basic substance. The answer he came up with was water, which of course is wrong, though he arrived at the answer by reason: water is everywhere, it surrounds the land, it comes down from the sky and springs from the earth, it can be a solid, a liquid and a gas, it is made up of many substances, etc.

Anaximander, who is said to have made the first map, went further. He did not believe in the water theory and suggested that the earth is freely suspended in space – a step in the right direction! He also formed the theory that life came from the seas and that man was originally a fish – very close to the truth. Later philosophers developed a theory of the atom, small particles of matter, of which everything is made up.

Aristotle was the greatest natural scientist. He established the principle of collecting facts before forming a theory, and he is rightly regarded as the founder of the study of biology. He examined the structure of living things and worked out a system of classification for plants and animals. He used the same methods in many other subjects – and there was hardly any subject on which Aristotle had nothing new and useful to say, from ethics to weather forecasting.

Medicine

The Greeks were the first to practise scientific medicine – as opposed to magic. The first great physician we know about, who realized that illness had natural causes and was not a punishment from the gods, was Hippocrates, who came from the island of Cos where he founded a medical school. He is supposed to have been the author of the Hippocratic Oath, a sort of code of practice for doctors, which at some medical schools is still learned by heart. Hippocrates taught the importance of careful observation and believed that a doctor had to consider the patient's general condition; he couldn't cure one part, said Hippocrates, without understanding the whole. Diagnosis – discovering the nature of the illness – could not be made without this knowledge, and diagnosis was the most important task a doctor had to perform.

Dead bodies were dissected in an endeavour to learn about anatomy, but operations were avoided as far as possible because besides being painful (there was no anaesthetic!) they were dangerous. Greek surgeons of course knew nothing about germs and infection. There were no chemical drugs, but herbal medicines were prescribed and doctors understood the importance of rest and exercise.

Asklepios (Aesculapius), the god of medicine, treating a patient. Asklepios seems to have been originally a hero rather than a god. But legend said he was a son of Apollo, and he was certainly worshipped as a god in Greece.

Mathematics and Astronomy

It is said that the most widely read book in history, after the Bible, is the *Elements* of Euclid, who lived about 300 B.C. The book contains the foundations of mathematics, although we think of Euclid mainly in connection with geometry. He introduced basic concepts like a line and an angle which he defined in relation to space. (Everyone remembers his definition of a line as having "length without breadth".) He used the deductive method (if A = B and B = C, then A = C), which had come down from Pythagoras who lived about two centuries earlier.

Ideas on astronomy owed something to earlier civilizations in Mesopotamia where

Archimedes' screw-pump, for carrying water up a slope, is still in use in rural parts of Egypt.

some constellations were recognized and named as early as 3000 B.C., but the Greek thinkers developed more rational ideas about the universe.

Aristotle believed that the Earth was stationary, though some Greek thinkers believed it moved. It is said that Aristarchus of Samos suggested in the 3rd century that the Earth moves around the Sun, but his written work is lost and his theory, nearly 2,000 years ahead of its time, has come down to us second- or third-hand.

In general the Greeks saw the sky as a turning, hollow sphere, with the stars embedded in it. It rotated daily causing the movement of the Sun from east to west. The individual movements of Sun, Moon and planets against the slower-moving background of the stars was explained by the theory that they moved in the space between the Earth and the heavenly sphere at a distance corresponding to their eastward movement around the heavens.

This idea of the universe is, like most Greek ideas, a very logical one. We now know it is incorrect, but the concept of a revolving heavenly sphere, not questioned until the 16th century, is still a useful model for looking at the universe.

Many of the greatest advances in Greek science and technology took place in the Hellenistic period, and are especially associated with the Greek colony in Alexandria (Egypt). Eratosthenes calculated the distance around the Earth. Archimedes invented a machine for irrigating and draining land, called the "Archimedes Screw". He also discovered (in his bath, tradition says) the principle that a body in water loses weight by an amount equal to the weight of the water it displaces, and calculated the value of π. Many inventions were made employing water and air pressure, even steam power, as well as the cog wheel. Ptolemy took the study of astronomy and geography to a level which was not surpassed in Europe until after the Renaissance.

Warfare

The Persian wars seem to have been the spur which motivated the great achievements of Classical Athens. In the same way it is possible to see the Peloponnesian War, in which Athens was defeated by the Peloponnesian League led by Sparta, as marking the end of that high period of civilization. Certainly, the defeat of Athens marked the beginning of the decline of the polis or city-state.

Perhaps we see the Peloponnesian War as more decisive, more important than it really was. The reason it looms so large in our minds is that we have a brilliant account of it by Thucydides, which makes what was an off-and-on Greek civil war into a universal moral drama.

Athens was first and foremost a naval power, and it was partly because the Athenians tried to take on their enemies on land

Left: A portrait of the great inventor Archimedes, as he was seen by an artist of the Renaissance.

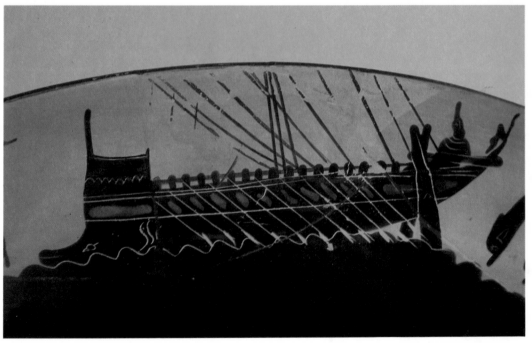

A 6th-century B.C. warship, powered by sail and oars. A man at the stern works the steering paddle, and porpoises follow behind.

A bronze, Corinthian helmet of about 500 B.C., which protected most of the face as well as the skull. When not actually fighting, the wearer pushed it to the back of his head, as in the statue of Athena on page 37.

made them vulnerable to ramming or to breaking up in rough weather. Yet they also needed to carry as many men as possible, because naval battles often depend not so much on manoeuvring the ships but on close quarters fighting which was rather like fighting on land. The oarsmen became soldiers, fighting with swords man to man.

Athenian captains understood the importance of concentrating their forces, which was mainly responsible for the famous Greek victory over the Persians at the battle of Salamis (480 B.C.). The Persian fleet was larger, but the Greeks lined up their ships across a narrow strait, with each flank protected by the rocky coast and more ships backing up the front line. The Persians were unable to bring enough force against the concentration of Greek ships and suffered many losses.

However, Phormio, an Athenian commander in the Peloponnesian War, defeated a Peloponnesian fleet at Naupactus (429 B.C.) by different tactics. His superior sailing powers enabled him to pin the Peloponnesians into a small space by encircling them. The enemy became more and more crowded together, and when a wind sprang up they began to bump into each other. Phormio then attacked, striking at the enemy commanders' ships first. And, Thucydides recorded, "such was the disorder that no one any longer thought of resisting, and they fled..."

The citizen soldiers of the Greek states normally fought in a pitched battle as a phalanx, a block of heavy infantry, about eight lines deep, who endeavoured to overwhelm the enemy by sheer force, armed with spears and short swords. They wore armour consisting of a helmet, including a face protector which could be pushed to the back of the head when not needed, a cuirass, or corselet, protecting the body, bronze pieces of armour called greaves which clipped on to the lower leg, and they carried a round or oval shield. They had archers in support, and chariots or cavalry,

that they suffered disasters in Sicily which led to the loss of most of their young men and the defeat of the city.

Greek warships such as the trireme were powered mainly by oars. They had a ram, a metal-clad projection at the bow, for crashing into enemy ships and breaking their oars. The purpose of arranging the oars in banks or rows one above the other was for strength. Oared ships are naturally narrow and shallow, and to build them too long but the mountainous Greek landscape was not well suited to cavalry.

The Greeks were fierce fighters but not great generals. The advances they made in so many other intellectual pursuits were not evident in their military science. They depended more on fighting power than clever tactics. At the battle of Marathon (490 B.C.), when they won a great victory against the Persians, they allowed the enemy to drive forward against their centre and then attacked them on the flanks, but this seems to have happened more or less by accident, not according to a plan. In general, when two evenly matched phalanxes met in battle, the line tended to move forward on the left and back on the right – the result of carrying the shield on the left arm. The Theban general Epaminomdas, one of the few clever tacticians, made the most of this tendency by deliberately placing his heaviest infantry on the left, while distracting the opposing Spartan phalanx with his better-trained cavalry. He won the battle, in spite of odds of over two to one against him, because the Spartan formation was broken up, making them relatively ineffective.

In spite of such defeats, the Spartan army was the biggest and the best. Spartan citizens were trained, as we have seen, in a military tradition: they were as good as, if not better than, professional soldiers. Other Greek armies were made up largely of peasants. Sparta also controlled a large area and could field much bigger armies than Athens and her allies, though Sparta could not compete with the Athenian navy.

Under Alexander the Great, a genuine military genius, the Greeks conquered the known world (though not all Alexander's soldiers were Greek). Their success was due largely to Alexander's creation of a fast-moving light-infantry force, to his use of heavily armed cavalry, as well as to skilful tactics. No less important was Alexander's organization of logistics. His staffwork was good, and his army always had its baggage

train nearby, its doctors, engineers and other auxiliaries in close attendance. Alexander also introduced "war engines", which hurled large missiles several hundred metres, in the role of artillery in battle. These had previously been used only when besieging cities.

Alexander's empire was a personal one which did not long survive his early death. Nevertheless, it had the effect of spreading Greek culture throughout the Mediterranean world – and beyond. This period is known as Hellenistic, which means "Greek" but distinguishes it from the culture of Classical Greece. The heirs of Hellenistic culture were the Romans, who within two centuries of Alexander's death, created a more enduring empire of their own.

Battle between Greeks and Amazons. The Amazons were a mythical race of warlike women. One of the Twelve Labours that Heracles had to perform was to capture the girdle, or sash, of the queen of the Amazons.

45

Index

Figures in *italics* refer to captions.